Memoirs of Peter

ARTHUR R. PITCHER

The Salvation Army
Supplies and Purchasing Department
Atlanta, Georgia U.S.A. 30329

I.S.B.N. # 0-86544-015-8

First Printing, May 1981
Second Printing, October 1981
Third Printing, March 1982

Printed in the U.S.A.

Available through Book Stores
or Salvation Army Supplies

Published by
The Salvation Army
Supplies and Purchasing Department
1424 Northeast Expressway
Atlanta, Georgia U.S.A. 30329

About the Author

A boyhood spent on the rugged shores of Newfoundland watching fishermen wrest a precarious living from the mighty Atlantic, and hearing their stories of storms at sea and struggles with wind and tide, provided the author of this little book with a keen insight into the life and character of Peter and with firsthand knowledge of the arduous toil and simple joys of the fisherman.

Of the turbulent sea and shifting sand, he found a counterpart in the man of the sea who, by Divine grace, was to become a rock of strength to the Christian Church.

When "Memoirs of Peter" first appeared as a series in The War Cry in 1980, the response with which it was received proved beyond doubt that "Peter" was speaking directly to hearts that throb with the same fluctuant emotions as those which plagued this fisherman disciple. The demand that his "memories" be published in a small volume was great – and this is the result.

Commissioner Arthur Pitcher was born in Winterton, Nfld. He attended Memorial University College and taught school for five years before becoming a Salvation Army officer in 1939. The commissioner has served in various parts of Canada, South Africa and the Caribbean, and is currently territorial commander of the USA Southern Territory.

D.G.H.

Foreword

It was on one of our annual furloughs near the Indian Ocean that the inspiration for "Memoirs of Peter" was born.

All day and into the evening the fishermen pursued their quarry, much as Peter and his friends must have done on sometimes peaceful, sometimes turbulent, Galilee.

As we sat in the twilight and looked out across the ocean, we read the Big Fisherman's story from the Gospel of Mark. Then, as He has so often, the Holy Spirit brought to light the struggles and victories of that man of the sea, whose counterparts I had known so long, and met so often on the shores of the Atlantic as on the shores of the Indian.

And as I mused, his memories began to take shape. I expressed them as they came and Betty wrote them down. It was an experience so rich and rewarding that it had to be shared. Thus the origin of *The Memoirs of Peter.*

May they be blessed in the reading as they have been in the telling, and, above all, may they be a tribute to the fisherman's best friend – the Stranger of Galilee.

Arthur R. Pitcher

Contents

Hope

I am Simon;
A man of sand was I.
For me, the very soul within me
Seemed to shake, and shift, and seethe.

I have seen the mottled sky
Move in troubled threat
Above the Sea of Galilee,
And plunge Gennesaret
Into sudden tempest.

So, upon my troubled soul
With warning less than cloud might give,
The spindrift swirl of doubt
Could suddenly descend.

I owned a fishing boat,
A stout and sturdy craft,
And fear and I were strangers;
Though I learned to treat
The elements with due respect.
'Twas not with fear my soul would tremble,
But with hope, and yearning long deferred.

When I had brought my shining catch to land
And held the Roman penny in my hand,
I writhed to know that Caesar's underlings,
Those aliens holding Israel in thrall,
Must have a share of what, by mighty toil,
I wrested from the often stingy sea.

The sight of Roman helmets,
The sound of Latin's mincing tongue
Stirred my Jewish blood,
Till I could curse them with the
Ancient wrath of Sinai,
And wish them in Gehenna
With their shields and swords and Caesar images!

And then like moonlight through the
Midnight clouds o'er Galilee,
The promise would break forth
To strangely comfort me.
Messiah!

One day for you and all your conquered,
Might-held nation
Deliverance will come,
And you will then be free.

11

The Call

I have seen the storm clouds rifted
With a beam of blazing light;
I have seen the sun in splendor
Drive away the shades of night;
But my soul has ne'er known ecstasy,
Nor known God's glory come to me,
As when on Jordan's bank there trod
The strong and sinless Son of God.

I stood unnoticed in the crowd,
And watched as from an evening cloud
A dove came timidly to earth.
As though that sky had given it birth;
It hovered o'er the Jordan stream,
While pristine white I saw it gleam.
And then upon that stranger fair,
Who stood in regal splendor there,
It paused; and from the cloud above
There came a voice, "My Son of Love
With pleasure now I give to men."

I watched Him, and within my heart,
I felt a pang of longing start.

I saw Him vanish o'er the hill,
The darkness deepened; evil seemed
To shroud Him, but I knew not then
What demon powers, what fiendish threat
Assailed Him in the wilderness.

But as for me, my nets were there;
And with a pang I scarce could bear
I took them up and sailed away
From morn till night, from night till day.
Yearning, burning, waiting, hoping;
And then with Andrew by my side,
I stood, and heard Him call my name
When back to Galilee He came.

All heaven was in that voice it seemed,
My visions now fulfillment deemed.
I followed Him, my nets behind,
My boat, my toil, I left them all;
For I had heard Messiah call.

Free!

The years have swiftly flown;
Yet clearer now than ever seems
The memory of those first glad days
Of wonder and companionship.

James and John, the sons of Thunder,
Left their father and their boats;
And together on the Sabbath
To the synagogue we went.

'Twas my custom, from my boyhood,
On the Sabbath day, to go
To the synagogue to worship;
And I truly learned to know
What the great "I Am" had purposed,
What His plan, what His design.

But I often sat in wonder
And confused, I sought in vain
To comprehend the mighty themes,
To compass all the just demands,
And hold within my memory
The fine requirements of the Law.

Sometimes the scribes themselves had pains
To reach agreement; and for me
'Twas hard to know which way to choose.
I needed firm authority;

And then, that day in Capernaum,
I saw that poor demon-possessed!
I had seen him oft, and noted how
He took men's pity, or their jest;
But that foul fiend within him knew,
That Sabbath morning, that my Lord
That evil thing in him abhorred;

That power which bound and fettered him,
That plagued, tore, and tormented him—
The Master knew that evil power
Had ruled his spirit, but that hour
He broke his chains and set him free.

And in my memory today,
I hear my newfound Master say
"Come out of him!" and he was freed.

And I was free as well, it seemed,
For in my Master's voice I heard,
And heard again through many a day,
The word for which my heart had yearned;
The word which held and strengthened me
Word of Divine authority.

From Mark 1:19-27

Light at Sunset

Between the hillside and the sea,
When I was young, I built my humble home;
And there, in love and harmony,
My wife, my little ones and I
Enjoyed the blessing of the Lord.

'Twas lonely, though, on stormy nights,
And since the day when
My wife's mother had widowed been,
She had come to share our home;
And in return she loved to serve.
And thus we dwelt so happily,
The children loved her as did we.

When Jesus climbed the little path
That led to my poor humble door,
I wished that it had better been,
That I could offer something more
To Him, whose honor I received.

For though I had but just begun
Discipleship with Him,

For me Messiah, King was He;
And yet His love did not disdain,
But marked with royal dignity
The cottage of a fisherman.

But when we came, in great distress,
My wife explained that raging fever,
Which in the summer sometimes swept
In unexpected suddenness
Across the coastal plain,
Today had laid her mother low;
And I must tell the Master so!

He smiled and reaching o'er the bed,
He touched her fevered hand;
Then, lo, anon, the fever gone,
She reassumed her loving task
And ministered to Him and us.

By then the sun was going down,
And, though a thousand sunsets I have seen,
None like that has ever been my joy.
From o'er the hills, through fields and vale,
They came, the poor, the weak, the frail.

Some whose eyes had long been closed
And could not scale my winding path
Except with help by those who sighted were;
Some on their litters, borne by friends;
Some hobbling on their crooked limbs;

And just beyond the crowd's last rim,
Their long, last hope their thought of Him,

The lepers huddled in their fear,
But dared not to my house draw near.

Then Jesus came through my front door,
Lifted His hands above the poor,
Turned radiant eyes toward the blind,
Made crooked limbs all straight again;

And, looking at those wretched men,
Crouched in their abject fear and dread,
Alien from home and friend,
He sent a message through the evening;
And looking where the sores had been
With wonder saw they, they were clean!

The sun went down o'er Galilee;
But ne'er again, it seems to me,
Has evening time been filled with light
As 'twas on that resplendent night,
When Jesus, Son of God and man,
Transferred to royal surgery,
The cottage of a fisherman.

From Mark 1:28-34

Conquest

'Twas not his trembling frame that broke his heart,
My neighbor of the palsied limbs!
But deep within the heart of him,
A goaded conscience tortured him.
An ancient venom, old as Adam's race,
Worked ceaselessly within his sinful mind.

The bitterness 'gainst God and Heaven,
The sharpened temper frayed by pain,
Which in frustrated heart is oft begotten;
The life of usefulness once seen,
Now lost, but ne'er forgotten—
And in the passing years, his soul
Caused him more writhing anguish
Than his body, uncontrolled,
Could e'er produce.

His neighbors, hearing news of Jesus nigh,
Constrained him to allow them but to try
To bring him within reach of healing touch.
They little knew how infinitely much
Their trembling friend Divine forgiveness sought.

Then, as Capernaum's crowded street drew nigh,
Their patient groaned the agony of one transcendent
"Why?"
So near to love's immortal miracle,
Yet how to reach the Master on this bed.

But neighbor love will find a way;
And they, with steady step, bore up the outward way;
Then, moving back the covering o'er His head,
'Twas quickly done, and there, before the Master lay
My neighbor, trembling more than e'en
His dread disease had caused him
With its bestial sway.

He shook with longings, yearnings unexpected,
And Jesus saw him there, and knew the grim despair,
The haunting conscience, and the sin-stained soul;
And thus with one forgiving word
The Savior, Son of God, made whole.

'Tis strange how men could see that lighted face,
Enraptured, and transformed by power and grace,
And then condemn the One who spoke the word;
But ever thus men criticized my Lord.

He turned, and looked at them with pity, not with
    scorn,
And with a gesture toward that man newborn,
But trembling still, He said,
"Whether is easier, to forgive a tortured soul
Or make a shaken body whole?
Take up thy bed, my friend, and go!"

And all the vanished strength of vanished youth
Responded to that word of love and truth,
And as he lifted high his now forsaken bed,
My neighbor knew disease had gone;
But even more, the plague within him was forever dead.

From Mark 2:1-12

My Brother

Discipleship with Christ had scarce begun,
When I faced mystery hard to understand.

I had seen the wretched cripple
Leave His touch with straightened limbs;
I had seen the blind man's eyes, agleam with light.
The fiend-possessed, now calm, with quiet mien
Had shaken off his spirit-binding chains;
The leper gazed with rapture at his body, now newborn,
And rescued from the living death
Of ignominious scorn.

What power was it that made my Master king
O'er demons, doubt, and dread disease?
His royal carriage, heavenborn,
Was proof to me, that with Him dwelt
Something beyond all human ken.

I asked, and sought, and asked again,
What gracious power His wonder wrought;
And slowly came to understand
That that which could man's mountains move
Was infinite eternal love.

In Him such power I perceived,
But, never could I have believed
That it could dwell in me, Simon, man of sand and sea.
Where could love in me begin?
I never could accept that I could love a publican!

Perhaps I could the gulf yet span
Between me and the leprous man.
The fault was not of human choice,
That made him what he was.

But publican! an Israelite,
Sold, groveling to the Roman might,
Accepting alien domination,
And making of its humiliation
Profit, gain, and hellish store!
Paying into the Roman hands,
And feathering his own wretched nest
With surplus beyond Rome's request.

When we passed by the custom house
I spat, and crossed the street,
As I had done so oft before;
Then I found I was alone.

My Master paused beside the custom door
And said to Levi, whom so often I had spurned,
What He had said to me by Galilee,
"Follow me" the invitation royal.

That night I found it hard
To yet be loyal

To Him, whom I had left my nets to follow.
But gradually I learned!
For Levi's ill-gained riches,
All his store, his home, his friends,
Position, evermore
Belonged to Jesus, and the poor.

And, as we learned to fathom one another,
Love filled my yearning heart,
And Levi, publican, became my brother.

From Mark 2:14-17

The Hand

I know the value of a man's hand.
How oft have I faced storm-tossed Galilee
And with my hands thrust straining oar
Into the seething billows
Until, protestingly but triumphant,
My boat has found its haven from the sea.

My hands have cast my nets into the oft reluctant
    deeps
And pulled them, strained and breaking,
    with their catch.
With these bare hands I've wrested livelihood
From tempest, toil and turbulence.

And oft on Sabbath morn when in the synagogue
The rabbi would exhort to thankfulness;
While others praised the Lord for house and lands,
For harvest richly given, or garnered grain,
I would lift my heart to God above,
And praise Him with my rugged love
For my strong hands.

One Sabbath morn when we had gone to prayer,
I saw among the gathered people there
A man whose hand no strength possessed.
Withered, obeying not the mind's behest,
Useless it lay, a thing of shame to him,
A token of frustration, dread and grim.

How dead may kindness be among the sons of men!
For there were those in synagogue that day
Whose hearts were not attuned to pity or to pray,
But sought for accusation 'gainst the Christ,
And held their heartless hedges of the law
More valued than the healing of that wretchedness
      they saw.

"'Tis Sabbath day; will He the healing act pursue?"
And Jesus looked upon him, and He knew
The evil thoughts that lurked within their hearts,
But with His gracious tenderness
Responding to the wistfulness
Of him whose need so clearly there presented,
He called him forth,

And standing by his side,
He faced those callous critics,
And demanded, "For what purpose has this day been
      given,
To come with base intent to synagogue,
And sit in judgment like some demagogue?
To nourish seething evil in the heart?
Or in God's house, where people come to pray,
To follow God, work righteousness,
And save men's lives on this His holy day?"

His eyes swept round that holy place with ire;
I saw the kindling of an inward fire
Of anger for the hardness of their hearts,
And then divinest love, and anger intertwined,
He matched with holy power the suppliant's
    yearning mind.

"Stretch forth your hand!" He said,
And suddenly,
Weakness gone, he found new strength,
And wonderingly stretched arm full length.
Then through a mist of tears he saw
A hand! a strong right hand!

Then, pausing gratefully to pray,
He blessed the Lord that Sabbath day,
And stepped out into life again,
To face his labor, hand made whole,
And healed as well a withered soul.

From Mark 3:1-5

My Boat and Me

The years, now held in gracious memory,
And any time which still is mine by grace,
Have been, and shall be dedicated
To pay installments on a still recurring debt.

Simon was my name, a man of sand was I,
And how the fire of love and trust,
The pressure of infinite love and grace,
Could take my shifting, windswept character
And change it into stone
Was more than I could see.

Yet in those first dear days by Galilee,
His love perceived the promise
And prophetically envisioned, e'en for me,
That after sandy, shiftless days had passed,
I would become Peter and would stand at last
Strong enough to form a vital part
Of the Kingdom He was building
For the human heart.

First He took my ship, my unpretentious boat,

And when the crowd had pressed Him to the sea,
He stood upon its moving deck
And made of my poor little barque
A pulpit from which wondrous tales He told.

A sower casting seed—the Kingdom seed—
And little birds, and thorn, and scorching sun
Undoing what the sower faithfully had done.
But harvest came, and thirty, sixty, hundredfold,
The seed received in willing hearts
Brought forth.

And, as His voice against the murmuring sea
Rose up as on the wave, then fell,
It seemed to me 'twas all a miracle.
My boat could never be as always it had been,
For He transformed it somehow on that day;

And when the crowd had all dispersed that night,
And Jesus took His path into the hills
To be alone to pray,
I sat and thought and wished—oh, how I wished!—
That just as He had changed, by using it,
My boat to something it had never been before,
So I might be by grace made worthy
Of "Peter," that new name which now I bore.

I look across the years, remembering now
What trouble, what despair I must have brought
To His dear heart before what He had sought
Could come to pass in me.
I loved Him, but I saw in Him a King.

How could I know redemption He would bring
By hanging on a tree?
Forbid it Lord! It shall not be to Thee!
And sorrowfully the sand was still in me.

It chafed His tender spirit, but He saw
That fires were burning that would weld
	the sand to stone.
How hot those fires!
Gethsemane! the judgment hall! fain would I
	forget,
But he forgave, and day by day, e'en yet,
Though many years have gone since Galilee,
It seems the grains of sand still fall away.

But by His power at breaking of the day,
This fisherman transformed by grace will be;
And I will be the rock He saw in me.

From Mark 4:1-20

Be Still!

You never could trust Galilee!
Sometimes a light and gentle breeze,
That caught the sunlight dancing
On its sparkling surface,
Would suddenly awake with fury,
And from circling hills,
Like demons suddenly set free,
The winds would sweep the lake
Into a boiling seething tempest,
With threat of death and danger in its power.

I saw the threatened storm signs in the sky,
I knew there would be tempest on the lake,
But fishermen have often risked the threatening storm
And, when the Master bade us, we agreed to take
Him in our boat and so set sail.

The Master had expended all He had,
And somehow I was comforted and glad,
To see Him cast a pillow in the stern;
And when I heard His measured breathing,
I determined that a careful watch I'd keep
That He might travel safely undisturbed.

But Galilee was to her nature true,
And as the night wore on,
A hurricane came sweeping o'er her face
And threatened ship and passenger and crew.
I shortened sail, and trimmed the little vessel
    to the gale,
But headway there was none, and mortal fear
Had gripped us all. The end was near.

I ne'er had seen a tempest such as this.
It seemed that all the devils of the lake
Spewed forth their wrath, some vengeance there
    to take;
And I could scarce believe that
Roaring wind and shrieking billows
Could fail to waken or disturb our Master's sleep.

At last the very sight of Him,
Sleeping there amid the awful din,
Unnerved me; and I shouted through the wind
"Dost Thou not care, O Master, that we die?"

And quietly He roused, and with a weary sigh
He stood, and as a monarch, mighty in command,
Bids subjects bow to His behest,
Or, as a mother lulls her fretful child
With loving but decisive words to rest,
So with rebuke He faced the storm,
And stretching majestically His hand toward the sea,
"Silence! Be quiet!" and obediently
The wind fell suddenly to calm,
The waves subsided, as a dog
When authority commands,

Will creep with whimper to his master's feet.
The storm was stilled;
But not the wild beating of my heart.

Who could this be, that with Creator's power
Could put the angry elements to rest?
I, who knew Galilee,
Knew that no storm had e'er before
Ceased with such suddenness as this.
"Something mysterious, something
        miraculous,
Something Divine is on the sea tonight."

Then He was speaking
"Why such fearful fright?
Where is your faith?" and we could only
        wonder.
What was it, this majestic, sovereign power?

And this I learnt that night on Galilee,
And years since then have shown its truth
        to me,
That having Jesus with you does not mean
A journey without storm;
But when your last resources have all failed,
When before the howling storm gusts you
        have quailed,
One word from Him and, lo, the storm will
        cease.
The tempest in the soul will yield to peace.

From Mark 4:36-41

38

Made Whole

What howling waste the human soul can be,
Brought from out the realm of Lucifer himself;
How spirit, made a vacuum
By lack of faith in God above,
Or barren of the influence of love,
Can find the empty spaces
Occupied by cursing and enslaving fiends.

In memory I see again
That morning in the country of the Gadarenes.
My Master, fresh from conquest of the sea,
Had scarcely left the ship
When wild, tormented shrieking from among the
    tombs
On Gadara's rugged mountainside
Caused Him to halt;
And terror shook us, revulsion and dismay,
So indescribably debased
The man, if man he might be called,
For manhood scarcely there had left a trace.

Authority had found him,
The law had seized and bound him,

But demon powers had snapped their chains,
And naught on earth could tame him.
We gazed one instant on that twisted, tortured face,
And swiftly fled to leave him
In his melancholy place.

Yet strange it was that somewhere
In the deep hidden regions
Of that devil-twisted mind,
Some faint surviving instinct
Sought for healing so divine;
And something once implanted by creation in the soul,
Recognized my Lord's divinity,
And knew that here was one last hope
To be made whole.

The demon powers revolted,
For reluctant were these fiends
To be expelled from that dark soul,
Whose very madness was their den of evil, shame
      and sin.
Torment us not, O Son of God!
But sovereign grace divine
Paused only to perceive, to hear
That tongue confess
That legions dwelt within.

The demons knew their hour had come,
And knowing that His power would then compel
To now vacate the soul their power for long
      had held
In slavery's ghastly chains,
Another dwelling place they sought,

And in their desperation driven,
Found bestial heart their only suitable abode.
But beast refused to live with that strange torment
Suddenly acquired,
And plunged them into darkness in the sea.

As storm last night had disappeared from
     Galilee,
So evil's darkness now had left
The soul, who Jesus had by grace set free.
A missionary he would become,
And tell the world his story;
But Jesus sent him back to home
To there give God the glory.

When through the days since that strange
     morn,
I find within me empty space,
Where fiends would harbor,
But for love and grace,
I've learnt to pray that every cavern
     of my soul
May be possessed of Him
Whose Presence makes me whole.

From Mark 5:1-14

Morning

"My little daughter, Lord!" the ruler cried;
And I knew then
That, though the crowds were thronging Him,
Though multitudes were pressing
With a myriad of needs that would not be denied,
My Master, with His healing touch, Jairus' cry
    would heed.

For the heart of His divinity
Could not hesitate to move,
When a child was in danger or in need.
Nor could the Son of Man refuse the urgency
Of a parent who for threatened child might plead.

And yet crowds—
They pushed Him, and they prodded Him.
Some came to see a miracle,
Some came with doubt, the cynical,
Some came because a hunger,
Or a longing broke their heart.

But in that milling throng was one,

Whose agony of hope
Defied her reticence,
Destroyed her hesitation,
Disdained the intervention of the throng,
And brought her, hand outstretched
With faith, to touch the Master's garment.
Her past had been a wilderness,
A dozen years of misery,
The pointless ministrations
Of incapable physicians,
And Hope!

But as she touched His garment hem,
As prayer and supplication welled within,
Virtue like a healing stream
Came rushing to her aid;
And knew that God had heard her as she prayed.

The Master too became aware
That some demand had reached His love,
And in the throng He saw her,
And to His feet He brought her,
And tenderly confirmed
That her faith had set her shackled body free.

But the messengers of gloom,
From the ruler's house had come,
And a lesson there I learn that comforts me—

That when prayers have seemed delayed,
And my heart is sore afraid,
'Tis not that God's forgotten my request;
But, while on the road to me,

44

His divinity may see
Other needs requiring healing grace.

"Your daughter's dead! Too late!" they said;
But Jesus laid His hand
On the shoulder of the father by His side.
"Trust Me yet," and I saw
That His love was not defeated or denied.

When, the wailing women driven
From that threshold dark with grief,
We stood with weeping mother,
And with father, wondering,
I saw radiance, and life,
And compassionate majesty,
That contended there with death for mastery.

Bending o'er the lifeless child
He spoke with accents strong but mild,
And death prepared to own His sovereignty.
He used the morning call,
Which her ears had often heard,
But now it called her to a newborn day.

"Come, little one, 'tis time to rise,"
And opening her lighted eyes,
She smiled at Him, and He smiled back at her.

Some days when persecution sore
Falls on His Church, and o'er and o'er
The death knell calls
And saints must helplessly obey,

My heart takes courage still,
For I know that Jesus will
One morning drive the shadows all away.

"'Tis time to rise," He'll say,
And in the dawning day
The saints will smile at Him
And He at them.

From Mark 5:22-43

Commissioned

The glory of the dawn on the sea of Galilee,
Catching cloud and mount and men
In the beauty of the morning,
Painting promise of the day
In a crimson, amber, indigo display.

Then, with the rising of the sun,
When the day has now begun
Disappearing, to new splendor giving way.

So John, the Master's herald,
Flaming prophet of repentance,
Had fulfilled his given task,
And before my Master's presence
Willingly his fame and honor gave away.

Now in Herod's loathsome dungeon
For the cause of truth he languished,
Till the one his truth exposed,
Taking vengeance in her hate,
Caused the prophet there to die
A martyr's death.

No more the crowds from hamlet, town and
        village came to stand
On the banks of Jordan,
And to be baptized.
And the Master knew His people
Had not yet been brought to God,
So He called us twelve one day
And sent us trembling forth
To spread the needed message
Far abroad.

To house, and field, and farm,
To the village in the mountain,
And the hamlet by the sea,
Two by two, we were commissioned
And "Where'er you go," said He,
"cast out demons, preach repentance,
Be a witness unto Me."

We were weak and inefficient,
Preachers we had never been.
Fishermen, and tax collectors,
Husbandmen, and servant men,
Zealots, doubters and some fighters,
But preachers never!

And yet we went at His behest,
And as we spake His Name,
The demon fled before us,
Divine grace and power possessed us,
And men, convicted, cast aside their sin,
And with repentance turned to God
In prayers and supplication.

Rejoicing we returned
Like warriors back from conquest on the field.
"O Master, as we spoke,
God broke the tyrant's yoke,
And we saw fiends and devils
To Thee vanquished yield."

Then He smiled so tenderly,
"You have served me well," said He,
"But your greatest joy must be
Not that devils fly before you in dismay,
But that in the Book of Life,
In my Father's house above,
Your names have been inscribed
By boundless love."

How well we should have known
That the Master was equipped for every task;
But the memory of victory,
Of His gracious power and glory,
Seemed to fade so very quickly,
And we quailed when faced with multitude to
        feed.

But He took the fish and bread,
Five loaves, two fishes, and the grace He said
Then sent us with the bounty from His hand.

We saw these hungry men so plentifully filled.
And then He called us to His side again.
He gave us each a basket,
And we gathered up the remnant of that feast,
And, lo, each basket was o'erfilled.

I never knew how it could be,
But even greater mystery
That we twelve men could fail to understand
That our Master's bounteous hand
Could supply us, as He fed the hungry crowd.

For me 'twas years with failure ridden,
And torn with inner strife,
Ere I saw the power hidden
In Him the Lord of Love, the Bread of Life.

From Mark 6:12-43

Cleansing

Those early days of fellowship with Jesus
Were filled with wondrous lessons day by day.
We, who had never known a teacher
Such as He was, failed to understand
That love and tenderness, divine compassion
Were of more importance
Than the multitude of "Hedges of the Law."

But we were common men,
Who oft had rushed from busy toil
To eat our hurried meals,
And catch the tide ere it had ebbed,
Or gather in our nets before a gale.
Thus oft the strict provision of the law,
The ceremonial washing it demanded,
Were overlooked or quickly done.

When we became disciples of the Master,
'Twas hard to change the habits of the years;
And when we sat at table, we'd forgotten,
Until we saw those pharisaical sneers.
He knew our hurt, as He knew all there was
    to know.

We saw the criticism, felt its sting.
He came to our defense, but more than that,
He made it clear that what He sought,
And that divine deliverance which He brought
Was God-designed to set the people free
From outward ritual and ceremonial cleansing,
To give instead a cleansing of the heart.

Fathers there were in Israel, and mothers too,
For whom the law demanded honor due;
But that same law which honest men condemned
For failure to attend its trivial tests,
Allowed the sons of those,
Who should have spent their last years quietly
In peace and venerable repose,
To give their sires their duty as a gift,
And hold them still in obligation,
Whose lives had for their children yet been
        spent.

And Jesus thrust before the keepers of the law
That Sinai-given, God-dictated precept
Demanding honor for the parent
And laying dire results on those who failed.

And with His tender spirit violated
By superficial teachers, thus He taught,
This vital truth that in the spirit,
Not in the outward form, lies righteousness;
That from a wicked heart untouched by grace
Proceed the sinful things which plague our race—
The thought unchaste, the senses uncontrolled,
The hate and bitterness,

The vile lasciviousness,
And all their wretched brood in word and deed.

And I, when next I took me to my prayers,
In deep repentance saw my soul's deep need.

Then, when we went with Him to Tyre and Sidon,
He showed by living type how from His heart
Could go to alien sorrow,
Love and blessing which could set the stranger
    free.
The Syrophenician woman who believed,
The boon of healing for her child received.

From coast of Tyre and Sidon
To the cities then He came,
That fringed the well-known coast of Galilee.
There deaf and mute were made to hear and
    speak.
And as we saw such miracles unfold,
Compassion leap from out His gracious soul,
We longed to have a spirit cleansed within,
That from triumphant lives released from sin
Might issue forth a power that would impart
Health for men's ills and cleansing for their heart.

From Mark 7:1-30

Revelation

As the gracious days unfolded
In the company of my Lord,
I struggled with a question
Which required an answer soon.

I had seen His mighty majesty,
His supernatural dignity,
His power to walk with simple men,
And glorify their common lives
By fellowship divine;
And yet I saw Him face the scorn
Of criticizing pharisees,
I saw His wisdom put to grief
Their infamous designs;
And sometimes in the still of night
I sat alone and tried
To comprehend what I had seen.

At first the answer was denied,
I could not understand
That God was there incarnate
In that serving Son of Man;
And yet I knew some mystic power

Which lay beyond my ken,
Was moving in that wondrous Lord,
Who with authoritative word
Could drive the demons from their lair,
Could dominate land, sea and air,
Could open beggars' blinded eyes,
And bid the palsied man arise,
Could feed a multitude with bread,
Claim lepers who were living dead;

And as He spake so graciously,
Yet with supreme authority,
There grew with me a great conviction,
That I, a man of shifting sand,
Within the hallowed footsteps trod
Of one who was the Son of God.

I feared to state what I believed,
But day by day the knowledge grew,
Until at last that question could
    unanswered be no more.

North from Galilee we traveled
To Caesarea Philippi.
The snowy heights of Hermon
Raised their head against the sky.
In that scene of lofty grandeur,
In a quiet rendezvous
Came this question,
"Whom do men think that I am?"

And we hesitated, stammered,
"Some say John, returned from death,

Some say prophet resurrected,"
Then He turned His eyes upon us,
With divine intensity,
And I felt that all within me
In that moment He could see.

"Thus I am to others," He responded,
And I knew that I must answer
His spirit-probing question.
"What am I to you?" said He.

The answer which I gave was born
Not in my simple heart;
It came, a flash of glory,
And I felt its power sweep o'er me.
It seemed, of all the race of men,
I, Simon, had been chosen,
To present the truth divine.
"Thou art Christ the Son of God," I said.

Vibrant that moment was
With truth beyond my wisdom.
He knew from whence it came,
Accepted it, and used my name—
The name that He had given me—
To promise that on such a word,
On such a faith should stand unshaken,
And bulwarked 'gainst the gates of hell,
His church, the dwelling of Emmanuel.

From Mark 8:1-30

Shadows

Life for me was full, adventuresome and free,
And day by day within us grew,
Among my friends and me,
A dream, a vision, an ambition.

Young men we were, and life was flowing at
      full tide.
With our Master's supernatural power,
His honor growing hour by hour,
Our eyes were on a kingdom,
Our desires were for a throne;
The royal son of David
And Eternal Son of God
Would weld in one the scattered bands
Of Zealots near and far,
And soon the royal emblem of our ancient,
      holy land
Would wave above an army
Under Christ's divine command.

We'd tear the Roman eagles
From their turrets and their towers;
The hated domination of our cruel overlords

Would bow before our legions,
Fly before our unsheathed swords.
Then, the kingdom firm established,
We close followers of the Lord
Would assume our rightful place
In the new and glorious realm.

Thus our mortal dream, but Jesus
Never talked of armed conquest,
And I could not understand
A strange look of pain He wore,
And the burden that He bore
For our immature ambitions
And our flashing bold desires.

Then just when all our hopes for Him
Were rising mountains high,
He looked at us—He looked at me—
And told us He must die.
Not in some far and future day,
With dreams all realized,
But in a shameful felon's death,
Rejected and despised.

I would not hear Him talk like this,
My spirit then rebelled;
"This shall not be to Thee, dear Lord,"
I cried. He turned and held
Me spellbound with a look
Which I shall ne'er forget.

He spoke to something deep within,
To greed, and avarice and sin,

And to that demon which designed
To thwart His spirit, now resigned
To die for man, He sternly said,
"Get thee behind me," and I knew
That 'twas to Satan that He spoke.

And from that day He talked of loss,
And slowly, faithfully He lifted
Before our dull and wondering eyes,
Not royal throne, but cruel cross.

"Who follows me must self deny,
And for my sake prepare to die.
The world's unreal evaluation
Must suffer full annihilation.
To gain the world and lose your soul
Would be a beggar's compensation."

We tried to fathom it, and blind were we,
For one triumphant word
In what He spoke escaped our observation,
And not till three days after Calvary
Did we remember that He promised
        Resurrection.

From Mark 9:31-38

Transfiguration

The mystery of suffering, of sorrow, pain
    and threatened shame,
The challenge of discipleship
Which called for sacrifice and death,
They burdened me.

And then one morning bright and clear,
With James and John, He beckoned me,
And from all others led us upward,
To climb with Him a lofty mountain steep.

We wondered as we climbed,
What revelation new,
What holy truth,
What lesson intimate and precious,
He had for our enlightenment.

How little did I know
That day should mark forever
Confirmation that my Master
Was the Son of God divine.

As we reached the mountaintop,

And our Lord passed on before us,
There came a supernatural influence,
A sense that we were lifted high,
Above all earthly sense and sound;
That we were on the threshold
Of a world we did not know;

And as we paused in awe and rapture,
Our Master there before us changed
Into a being, pure, seraphic,
Like Gabriel in his shining garments,
Like one who through the distant ages
Had come to prophets and to sages.

In His raiment, white and glistening,
There transformed before our eyes,
Stood our Lord in heavenly splendor;
And I still remember how
Instinctively we knelt before Him,
Fearful, trembling, and unworthy.

Glorious in His majesty,
Bearing word of destiny,
As the light that shone on Moses
In the mount of Sinai;
So His glory all resplendent
Fell on James, and John and me.

When we lifted up our eyes.
We were filled with new amazement;
For where He had stood alone
He now had gracious company.
From where they came we could not tell,

But in our hearts by some strange revelation
We knew them, and our spirits quailed with fear.

The dignity of prophet-shepherd
Covered one as with a mantle,
The hands that once had held
The mighty tables of the law,
A glory similar to this;
He bore the stamp of honor, still revered
By all our race through many generations.

We knew that Moses, heaven-sent,
Stood there beside our Master.
The fiery chariots of the Lord
Had swept into the heavenly glory
Long centuries past, Elijah, famed in Israel's
    story.
The mountain man of fire and word
Now shared that mountain with my Lord.

I felt like some ill-come intruder,
And I, who but short days before
Had spurned the thought
Of death and loss,
Now heard with wonder and amazement
These two of Israel's greatest sages
Discuss with Him, the Lord of ages,
The scope and meaning of the Cross.

Suddenly my trembling voice
Broke into conference sublime.
I knew not what to say or how,
But felt that we should shut away
Such splendor from our human eyes.

"Lord let us make three tabernacles,"
I whispered, and He smiled at me,
As oft He did when blundering
Galilean tongue betrayed me.

Then, like the thunder rolls o'er Hermon,
Another voice majestic, glorious,
Spoke from a cloud that slowly gathered
Around the summit of the mount,
"This is My Son by Me beloved."

And all o'erwhelmed and faint with fear,
We sensed God's majesty draw near.
The cloud came down;
We entered it, and thought if we should live
     beyond it.

Then silence came upon the hill,
The voice of God and seer were still,
And when we dared to lift our eyes
Our Master stood, all shorn of rapture,
Bowed head submissive to His Father.
"Please tell the story not," said He,
"Till Son of Man is glorified."

I look back through the mist of years
And e'en as now the tale recount
I seem to hear again that voice,
To see again that shining glory,
Hear again redemption's story,
Discussed by Moses and Elijah
With Jesus in the holy mount.

From Mark 9:1-10

Little Ones

From the glory of transfiguration,
We came back to find a father torn with grief.
He had thought that those
Who fellowshipped with Jesus
Must have caught His mighty power
To help and heal.

He came, clutching by his hand his little son,
And he begged from them the miracle of
      healing.
His little lad was taunted and tormented
By a power, grim and sinister, within.
Speech had gone and writhing, foaming torment
Had threatened life itself.
And day by day the father watched his boy
Grow wan and helpless, and in weakness pine
      away.

Now Jesus ever found His heart
Respond to need, or fear, or illness in a child.
He loved them so,
And we who, occupied with wild ambitions,
Of kingdom, thrones, dominion and a sword,

Who saw His path a royal way to glory,
Would turn away the children with a word.
Too busy now to hear your fretful wailings

Too busy now to laugh, or pause to play,
Our hearts had not yet caught
His humble royalty.
Not only so, but faith so often stumbled
Before the mysteries of pain and tears.

When, from out the cruel way of sorrow,
This father came with child, in such dire need.
Disciples failed, their power quailed.
The truth was they had never learnt to take
Men's sins and sorrows on a burdened heart,
Nor in their prayers had learnt to plead
With anguish,
Or even sacrifice the call to appetite,
To share with those who could not cope with
        pain.

Thus helpless stood they,
As the Master from the mountain
Came down to meet them in the plain;
His kindly heart, compassion-ridden,
With mighty word that little lad set free.
"O pray," He said, "and fast,"
If you would conquer demons
Torturing little children such as he.

So strange it seems, in restrospect to ponder.
That we could close our ears, and blind our eyes,
And choose to miss His teachings of the Cross.

We squabbled on the road,
Pressed our petty claims to fame potential,
And fought inglorious battles for position
In the kingdom, which our conquering Lord
    would build.

When we came to rest beside Him in the
    evening,
I saw again the pain, I recognized
And knew that He had heard our conversation.
I quailed before the sorrow in His eyes.

A little lad was running in and out,
With laughter, and Jesus caught him as he
    passed Him by,
And sat him on His knee.

Looking at us with divine condemnation
"If you would have me as your friend and ally,
If you would walk with me along life's road,
Learn to receive a child like this," He said.
"Desiring to be first in heaven's kingdom,
 Reveals a spirit alien to its cause.
 Tis those who cast aside selfish ambition,
To whom the kingdom which I build belongs."

How could I ever have forgotten?
How hard it was for Him to make us see
That His divine and wondrous power was this;
And clear it should have been to James and
    John and me,
That righteousness could be with glory crowned,
Could talk with Moses and Elijah, on a
    mountain,

Could be accorded God's own acclamation,
And yet could challenge demons in a boy,
Relieve a father's agonized distress,
And sit upon a boulder in a market,
And hold a little lad upon His knee.

From Mark 9:17-37

The Challenge

The way toward Jerusalem
We trod reluctantly.

Now, as in light of memory,
I see that winding way,
My heart rejoices to recall
How hour by hour, and day by day,
Along each lane and desert road,
The people crowded eagerly,
And with compassion He would turn,
And with His wisdom infinite,
Would deal with problems intricate,
The sanctity of marriage vows,
The blinding quality of love,
The value of a little child.

And then one day in desperation,
By yearning driven, running came
A seeker for eternal life.
"Good Master," cried he, "please explain
How I Thy bounty may obtain."

And Jesus loved him tenderly,

And loving him, could not present
Him with a hope of transient peace.
To Sinai He led him first,
To Decalogue to Moses given:
These are the attributes of life.
"To keep them, Master, have I striven."

Then Jesus pulled aside a curtain
And showed him man in direct sorrow,
The hungry, sick, and weary driven,
Men without hope for earth or heaven,
And by His gracious love compelled,
The seeker that poor world beheld.
Then measured he his own position;
He sought for life—eternal life,
But held within his grasping hand
That affluent world he could command.

"These treasures you must lay aside,
And be prepared to suffer loss,
And bear an ignominious cross,
Compassionately feed the poor,
And follow Me forevermore."

He hesitated, standing there,
Two worlds his challenge, could he dare
To pay the price which life demanded?
He turned, and then, through misty eyes,
The Master saw him take the road
And turn his feet away from God.

"How hard," said Jesus, "is the way
From worldly wealth to endless day.

A camel through the Needle's Eye,
When stripped of all he bears, may go;
But they who trust in worldly treasure
Have difficulties without measure,
To throw aside that which they trust
And walk in faith, which yet they must
Who would be saved."

I listened, watched, and then elated,
Remembered all that I had left,
My house, my family, and my boat;
And proudly I presented proof
That I had loved Him, loved enough
To leave my world to follow Him.

And patiently He smiled at me;
You've left your house,
Your brothers, sisters,
Your father, mother, wife and child,
Your earthly store, but, lo, I say
Now here below an hundredfold,
And in the realms of endless day
The glories of eternal life,
Will I your sacrifice repay.

And then while still we spoke of loss,
He sought to make us understand
What sacrifice He came to give.
And once again before us thrust
The shadow of the waiting cross.

From Mark 10:17-32

Status

What wretched selfishness may dwell within
    the human heart!
With our faces toward Jerusalem,
His suffering, and a cruel death,
We fought for station and position.

James and John, ambitious men,
Who felt that leaving all behind
To share the penury and loss
Of following the Christ,
Leaving father Zebedee
To find a substitute for two strong men
Who now were far from ship and Galilee;
Surely, such sacrifice demanded
Some special recognition.

So, when they found a moment
Convenient to ask,
They made their bid for glory,
Asked for preferential status
In the kingdom that should be.

John told me later, when the mists had all
    been cleared,

How the eyes of Jesus
Looked him through and through, then gazed
At some hidden far horizon;
And though they did not know it then,
His eye was on a bitter cup,
And hate of bitter men.

"A baptism waits Me yonder
Such as eyes have never seen,
When through fire and pain and broken heart
I ford a Jordan in full flood,
With sacrifice and tears and blood.
Are you prepared to share that fate?"
They could not realize the truth,
But thought that parable He spake.

"O yes, the baptism we will share,
The cup of sorrow we will take,
If when You mount Your heavenly throne,
And claim the kingdom for Your own,
We're there to share Your glory."

"Ah yes," the Master said, "the cup
I drink in sacrifice you'll share;
The baptism of blood and tears
On naked flesh you'll bear;
But in my Father's hand remains
The accolades of victory.
His love and wisdom will decide
Who worthy are to sit beside
Your Sovereign on His throne."

When we had heard how selfishly
These two disciples sought

To supersede the other ten,
All of whom sacrifice had made,
We let our anger rise within us.
I scarce can now believe
That 'twas on Calvary's road we argued thus.

But Jesus graciously portrayed
The tokens of authority
That marked position in His kingdom.
Not those who petty tyrants are,
Not those who use the grace vouchsafed
To make them rulers of their brethren;
But he who dons a servant's apron
And humbly seeks in Jesus' name
To minister, e'en to be a slave.
These the credentials that He gave
For those who honored were to be
In His new kingdom.

And as we watched His kindly deeds,
How patiently with love He served,
How mind and heart and will He gave.
The lesson that He taught grew plain,
And on through penury and pain
We pressed, not for a worldly crown,
Nor for vain glory or renown,
But that beyond the pain and loss,
The sting and stigma of the Cross,
We might lay at His pierced feet
Some spoil of battle nobly won,
Some gains of whitened harvest wheat;
And that when day at last was o'er
We might be with Him evermore.

From Mark 10:35-45

Majesty

Though through a cloud of pain I see it now,
Remembering how the pain and sorrow,
Shame and bitterness
Closed the week so gaily there begun;
Yet, even now, I hear again the songs,
And see the children dance,
And watch the palm trees spread,
While with us all creation seemed to sing
"The day has come!" We thought
The pain and grief that holds our Lord enslaved,
The tyrant's power, the manacles of Rome
Would now be shaken from our smitten land.

"O come, all Israel's sons, and crown your king!"
So royal He looked, as plodding on in lowly
            majesty,
Upon the little beast, whose fears He quelled
By loving touch as loud the chorus swelled,
"Hosanna! Hosanna!"
I thought my heart would burst.

And then, around the mountainside
We came to see

Jerusalem, the city of the king,
Her walls and palaces, her shrines and gilded
      tombs,
And, shining over all, the Temple's golden dome;
And, running close to where the Master's donkey
      trod,
I turned to speak of our dear house of God.

But then the words were stopped upon my
      tongue,
For as His eyes that well-loved city swept,
My Lord, my Savior bowed His head and wept.
"Jerusalem, O Jerusalem, men have died in
      thee,
Prophets, messengers, sent to warn and comfort
      thee,
And I have come, the last of that great line,
Yearning thee to claim as God's and mine.
Wings of love outspread to shelter thee,
But you were blind, My grace you could not see,
And now, too late, I hear the fearful knell
Of judgment, of a yawning hell
That opens in a day of visitation
And blots thee out, as land, people and nation."

Into the Temple courts He came,
Majestic in His splendor.
The same divine authority
That brought to heel old Galilee,
Now laid its mighty power again
On merchants, moneychangers, men
Who made of Temple courts
A thoroughfare for trade.
I saw them quail before His glance,
I saw a fig tree wither at His word.

My heart grew fearful at such majesty,
And challenged to confess
The source of such authority,
By scribe and priest,
By elder and by Pharisee,
He stood unawed, unbending, very Lord,
His life now threatened,
But His power His word.

How is it, even yet I cannot see,
That one short week
Beyond that glorious day
Should see us scattered,
We who now stood by Him.
Shame, O shame!
It heard my lips deny Him.

From Mark 11:1-18

The Vineyard

In glowing green the vineyard lay,
Under the midday sun;
And through its avenues there moved
The vinedressers, the working men;
And Jesus gathered us around
And told a story so profound
That only now that years have passed,
And when the time is coming fast
When I shall at His feet present
The harvest of these laboring years,
Can I describe its full portent.

A vineyard set and hedged,
Prepared for harvest, rich and dear,
Was to the husbandman let out.
But day by day and far away
The owner of the vineyard thought
Of burdened vine, of ripening sun,
And when the summer's work was done,
He sent his servants to receive
The vineyard tribute to him due.

There at the vineyard gate he stood

And sought to represent his lord,
And urged them thus to recognize
His master's honor, to accord
Him fair return for what was his.
The vinedressers his honor scorned,
And as the servant pressed his claim
Their anger turned to threat,
Then blows, and empty-handed he returned.

Another servant, still another;
One staggers home with head all bruised,
And one returned upon a bier.
They gave, they sought, they made their plea
But fruit or honor, tribute free,
Of these none brought
To him whose love had planned the vineyard.

What now to gain the honor due
Could love or patience further do?
"My son, my only son," said he,
"He lives with me, he loves with me,
He bears my name, my nature wears,
When he before the gate appears
They'll honor him as sent from me."

So to the vineyard son and heir
Came to present, came to declare
That he whose claims they had disowned
Was willing yet in love to spare
If they allegiance would declare,
By fruit and tribute, recognition,
Disclaiming thus self's vile ambition.
The son thus came, and thus he died,

For claim of sire and son denied
The keepers of the vineyard fair.

'Twas when I saw a cross uplifted
And heard a heart by sorrow rifted,
While on that cross my Master died,
That I at last came to perceive
What scarce my heart dared to believe,
That God the Father so loved men
That when their vilest deeds were done,
When honor, tribute, homage, love,
Were by His servants yet refused,
He loved them still, and by that love
Sent forth to die His only Son.

From Mark 12:1-11

Giving

"To Caesar that which Caesar's is"—
It took us by surprise!
To God we owned our fealty due,
But Caesar! what we gave to him
Extracted was by tyranny,
Or so at least it seemed to me;
And when the men from Herod's party
Came questioning Him, uneasily
We waited for His sage reply.
To Caesar tribute, how, or why?

He took a penny in His hand,
And as the sun shone on its silver,
Fear gripped me, I could scarcely breathe.
His answer boded good or ill
For all of us.
Deny the publican his custom,
Penalty was swift and sure;
And yet his privilege to demand it
A freeborn Israelite would abjure.

But Jesus knew the awful struggle
That tore the patriot heart asunder;

He also knew the heaven-born claim
Of righteousness, and so it came,
That Herod's men could find no fault
With judgment so divine and fair—
To Caesar his, to God His own,
And they marveled at the wisdom
He displayed.

Values to our Master
So often seemed to be
So different from our calculations,
For He deigned to see
That beyond the piece of silver
Good or evil worked their way;
One to make men cold and callous,
The other love's dear debt to pay.

We were standing by a column
In the Temple court one day
When, with pomp and ceremony,
Scribes and Pharisees drew near.
With golden gift, assured of suitable applause,
With due acclaim and fine display
They brought their fee of riches
To the Temple treasury.

When all applause had died away
And they with honor had departed,
A woman clad in widow's garb,
All trembling, diffident, timid came,
Holding her small mite with shame;
Looked right and left to satisfy
That no appraising human eye
Could see that meager gift she brought.

And yet as in the treasury
The coin was dropped, she knew
That widow's mite was all she had,
And Jesus saw it too.

No plaudits honored that small gift,
But turning to us as He stood,
Divinely He acclaimed that token
Of love, from heart by sorrow broken,
The gift of all her earthly store.
"Behold," He said, "she giveth more
Than all who have preceded her."

I pray with fervor day by day,
Dear Christ, whate'er may me befall,
Help me, like her, to give my all.

From Mark 12:13-17, 41-44

Farewell

'Tis strange how in a lifetime,
Marked by sunshine and by storm,
One week, one day, yea e'en one hour,
Can stand like Hermon, far above
The minute foothills of the years.

'Twas thus in that last week
That brought my Master to His Calvary,
And then beyond the reach of death
To guerdon of immortal life.
Looking back across the twisted years,
'Tis strange how now pervades dear memory's
    air,
The perfume from a broken alabaster box.

She never knew—how could she know?—
That woman with the scarlet-named repute,
That as unfolding centuries
Would tell again the story of that week,
Her gift of love, her outpoured ecstasy,
Her gift extravagant,
Her wasted balm, would treasured be,
Love's prodigality,

The incense of a tomb,
But breathing everlasting life's perfume.

He knew it so, my Master knew,
And stilled the critic's caustic condemnation.
When we the fragrance of that perfume knew
    again,
Out hearts were broken under Calvary;
But He could see beyond the aromatic tomb,
And knew that in the memory of the years,
Her tribute to His life and love would stand
As a wondrous token of His royal command
Of life eternal, life wrested from the conqueror
In the garden tomb.

But e'er that revelation came to us,
He drank His farewell cup with us,
He prayed with us,
He sang with us,
Then crossed the Kidron brook with us,
To drink the gall of death for us,
And loving us unto the end,
Promised the Paraclete He'd send
To stay with us.

That supper, how shall I forget?
"Betrayed am I," He said,
And yet we could not feel
That human heart could condescend
To stain his hands and soil his soul
By selling thus the Son of Man.

And as for me, beneath the table's rim

I clutched my sword and vowed my loyalty to
   Him.
When cup came round, though naught I
   understood
Of what He meant, "This is My Blood,"
I quaffed it down and made a secret vow.

When bread was given, and "This is My Body,"
Solemnly He spoke,
Then as for me, I ate that bread,
And for the strength I prayed
That I might let Him know
That I, Cephas, the stone, would never be afraid.

He looked at me, and through the intervening
   years
I feel my heart stand still again.
"Before the cock crows twice, thou shalt deny
   Me thrice."
Am I but yet a man of sand?
Will I indeed at fear's command,
Go sniveling like a coward knave?

"Come, let us go," and neath my cloak
My sword I clutched, no word I spoke.
And thus through pitch black night
We strode across the little brook
And through the olive trees with Him
To bitter, dark Gethsemane.

From Mark 14:3-9, 17-32

The Vigil

We stopped beneath the olive trees;
And is it but the memory
Of all that shrouded us that night
That makes me feel that never night
In all the history of the world
Had been so dark,
So filled with evil shadows,
As that night neath the olive trees,
In that "place of the winepress,"
Gethsemane?

A prophet long before had cried,
"I have trodden the winepress alone,"
And yet at darkened glade He paused,
And out of the twelve He took us three,
Just James, his brother John and me.

His human heart wished not to be alone;
And though there was a midnight place
That only He could tread, He trusted us
That while in agony, He said,
"Remove the cup, O Father, if it may be Thy
    will."

We three so near would stay that hour,
But we had neither will nor power
To share His lonely vigil.
Another heard Him as He prayed,
And gave to us His broken words,
"Father, the cup, please take the cup!"

What was it the watcher did not see?
Did angels clear the midnight sky,
And whisper comfort?
Did strength from out the Father's heart,
And love, and tenderness, and grace,
Attend the sufferer's agony?

I do not know, for I was fast asleep,
But he who heard could only say
That there was in His prayer a change:
"Father, Thy will be done, the cup I'll take."

Twice had He left His place of prayer
To find us sleeping;
Twice had He called us,
Found no watch had we been keeping.
I who bore my futile sword
Had thrice already failed my Lord.

"Come now, the hour is close at hand,"
And through the trees that hostile band
Led on by Judas, one of us,
One who had broken bread with us,
One whom the Master fed with us,
Approached Him now with traitor kiss.

Until the sun goes out in darkness,
Until the stars and moon are dead,
Never will man see kiss like that,
Mankind in that one base encounter
Revealed the abyss of his sin.

But who am I to pass such judgment?
I struck one blow in His defense,
Then scurried back amid the shadows.

They took Him, and at some safe distance,
Keeping their marching torch in view,
I crept behind the staggering Christ.
Where now my confidence, my trust?
And so, in fearful ignominy,
I passed into the high priest court,
To face my own Gethsemane.

From Mark 14:32-46

Denial

How often man would lay away
The record of one bitter day,
Expunge the writing, clean the slate;
Yet such desire oft cometh late.
I write with sorrow in my heart,
And e'en as now I tell again the story,
The salty tear-drops start.

'Tis not because I have not been forgiven,
But as through all the years in love I've striven
To live for Him, to love for Him,
And soon perhaps to die for Him,
I've yearned to erase the bitter memory
Of that grim morning in the judgment hall.

'Twas cold, the winds of dawn
Came shuddering o'er the hill,
The dews of night and garden
Had left me with a chill.
And so, within the court
I found a place where I desired
That the shades would hide my face,
While heat from soldier's brazier

Would cure my shivering ague.

My body might be warmed, but icy winds of fear
Swept through every cavern of my soul.
I saw, as through a haze,
My Master standing there.
I heard the filthy tongues of men
Their infamy declare.
I heard them tell how He had said
A temple He would build in three short days,
If that fair house on Zion's hill
His followers should raze.

He looked at them but spoke no word,
I feared for Him, my silent Lord.
But evil though the truth must be
I feared for Him, but more for me.
I saw the rolling waves of hate,
And knew for Him 'twas now too late
To save from venomed priestly lair.
My soul went swirling down the eddy
Of complete and numbed despair.

Lost in my awful contemplation,
I scarcely noticed that a maiden standing there
Was scrutinizing me with curious mien,
Until I heard her voice,
"Thou too wert with that man, that Nazarene."

Fear gave the answer, God knows, not my will,
And through the years it seems
I hear it echoing still:
"I do not know Him, know not what you say!"

I left that fire and tried to hide myself away.
Across the distant hills faintly I heard
A cock crow.
Something in me shuddered.
And then from out the shadows,
Another maiden's face,
Another maiden's question, hastened my
    disgrace.

"Lo, here is one of them," she said.
"Not so," I cried.
Could shame be dead within me that I answered
    so?
The very words I spake,
The very accent that I used gave me away.
And those that stood there
Heard my Galilean tongue;
And when they to that fact referred,
A trapped and hounded man of sand
Emerged from out the new dimension
That Jesus Christ had given me.

And from my Galilean tongue
Poured forth such words
That three bright years had never heard.
The filthy language of my past,
The oaths that marked those distant days,
Before His call by Galilee.
And while the words were still upon my tongue,
The morning cock sent forth
His summons to the day.

They took my Master, leading Him away,

And as He heard that sound
He turned and looked at me,
And my heart broke!
For in His look my agonizing soul could see
Pain and sorrow, agony.

What should I do? take Judas' course
And end the drama here and now?
I rushed from out the judgment hall,
I found a place where none could see,
And through that dawn I wept such tears,
Poured forth such prayers,
And while they dragged my Lord away
Prostrated in my grief I lay
And wished to die.

From Mark 14:53-72

Submission

The morning of that fateful day
Broke on my soul,
Where all the fiends of evil
Mocked my failure and my shame.
But though my heart was broken,
I could not turn away
From that grim drama
Which my stricken Lord
Had chosen thus to play.

The Roman, Pontius Pilate,
Was a ruler among men;
But indecisive, fear-inspired,
The victim of a mob's mad whim.
I, who had failed my Master, found
It in my heart to pity him.

How could he know that silent God,
Who stood before him in His shame,
Was mightier than the might of Rome?
How could he know that in His name
A myriad souls would yet arise
To build upon the ruins of empire
A structure higher than the skies?

He thought he tried a Nazarene
For some obscure and Jewish crime.
He did not know himself was tried,
Not only then but for all time.
"Art thou the Jewish King?" he asked,
And Jesus said "'Tis as you say"!
And thus rang up the opening curtain
Of the Savior's judgment day.

Priests and soldiers might deride Him,
But this man, who had denied Him,
Loved Him, yearned to have Him know
That in love he stood beside Him
As they mocked and jeered and cursed Him.

In his dungeon vile Barabbas,
Hourly waited for the cross,
Till a soldier stood above him,
Snapped his chains and set him free.
Thus mankind has chosen violence,
Murder, rape and robbery,
Rather than the love brought to them
By the Man of Galilee.

Pilate's fateful hesitation,
Broke before the mob's insistence.
White-faced, weak and self-despising,
He turned his back upon the Christ.
And left Him to the soldier's scourgings.

They mocked Him,
Clothed Him with a mud-stained purple,
Crowned His head with plaited thorns,

Shouted insults to His kingship,
And spat upon Him;
And when all was done,
Led Him out to crucify Him.

When it seemed I had reached the uttermost
    depth,
One other shade of shame swept o'er me,
On the grim morning of the Cross.
I, who should have stood beside him,
I, whom cowardice had broken
Stood among the crowd that thronged Him
And with agony beheld
That another, a Cyrenian,
But a man who bore my name,
Took the Cross from bleeding shoulders,
Bore it to the place of shame.

I, who with the frenzied crowd
Walked the paths of skull-shaped hill,
As I tell the wondrous story
Still can feel the shadow o'er me.
Though His grace my shame expunged,
I shall only prove my sorrow
In the day my footsteps follow
To the sacrificial cross.

From Mark 15:1-21

The Veil

How oft I stand at Golgotha!
The years have but intensified the pain,
The agony, the sorrow and the shame
Of that imperishable day.

The morning sun illumined Calvary,
And etched in bold relief
Three crosses 'gainst Judean sky.
On two were men who, by the law
Of justice, were condemned to die.
The seer Isaiah prophesied
The manner in which Jesus died.

Identified with men was He,
He shared transgression's infamy;
But as I saw Him there that day,
It seemed to me that venomed hate
And railery and insult vile
Spared the transgressors by His side,
And did my sovereign Lord deride.

"Destroyer of the Temple, Thou,

Descend that cursed gibbet now!"
Priests still their enmity express
And, mocking thus, do Him address:
"Christ, king of Israel, come down
And prove Thy right to wear a crown!"

Thus evil word and cruel jest
Befouled the lips of sin-cursed men;
Until at last the sun refused
To longer light that spectacle
And hid its face.
She dropped the curtain of the night
While it was still midday on Calvary.

From out the hideous darkness
Came a cry
Which I shall hear forever till I die:
"Eloi, Eloi, lama sabachthani,
My God, my God, why hast Thou forsaken me?"
I never knew till then
The cost of love's eternal quest.

How could I know,
How could man ever know
What dark gehennas trod that sacred soul?
What caverns of man's evil, lust and sin
His spotless soul was caused to grovel in?
He came to be the Savior of the lost,
Identifying with them at such cost
That Father's face from His was turned away.

But as I watched and listened, sorrow riven,
Up from those ghastly depths

His soul arose.
And in His Father's arms like tired child
He dropped at last in death's sublime repose.

The Temple veil of scarlet, purple, blue,
From top to bottom was riven.
And men, long shut from out the grace
Of seeing through the veil their Father's face,
Because of that grim hour on Calvary
Could now approach in faith the holy place.

The long day closed,
The paschal moon arose,
While in the twilight Joseph came
And gave his family tomb to Him.
In narrow bed my Savior lay,
The stone had shut Him from our sight
And quietly we left the garden tomb
To death's vile sting, grave's victory, and night.

From Mark 15:22-47

The Dawning

Do you know what it is for the sun to go down
On a backslider's soul, paying terrible cost?
On discipleship broken, eternally lost?
Do you know what it is to stand neath a cross,
And know that you should be sharing that loss,
That pain, that grief and that sorrow?
Do you know what it is to look back at a night,
With no promise of any tomorrow?

I am Peter, a man of sand,
Who had felt the touch of the Master's hand;
And just as the sand was turning to stone,
I walked from His presence, broken and lone.
For I had denied Him!
Disciple? Not I!
I had forfeited all
And then saw Him die.

But the morning broke fair
O'er the garden of death;
And swift on the wings of sublime victory,
Angels swept down and opened that grave.

Broken death's power! now mighty to save,
He stepped from the tomb, my Master and Lord;

The angels remained with triumphant word.
To women amazed and affrighted they said,
"He is not here in the realm of the dead,
But living, go tell His disciples," said they,
"To rendezvous with Him, near dear Galilee."

And then such a word a treasure shall be
As long as remembrance is given to me,
A word for my wandering, a balm for my woe,
A word for the broken of spirit to know.

E'en now recalling, through many long years,
I cannot express it, except through my tears.
"And Peter," He said, and back from the dead,
From my grave of backsliding, I arose and I fled
On feet winged with fire,
With a heart overflowing.

And now as I wait for the wings of the dawn,
That shall herald for me
A new day with my Master,
I think of that morning,
Arms spread to the world,
When He bade us go forth,
With Love's banner unfurled.

The prison has glowed with a bright burning ray;
The nights have been filled with the glory of day;
The stripes have been precious

When suffered for Him;
And soon, unworthily, this man of sand,
Rock-hewn at last, by his Master shall stand.
I shall pass the same portal that He passed for
  me,
And in that new country His servant shall be.

From Mark 16